ZooBorns!

zoo babies from around the world

Andrew Bleiman * Chris Eastland

BEACH LANE BOOKS
New York * London * Toronto * Sydney * New Delhi

For my parents, for taking me to the zoo *a lot*—A. B.

For Eloise and Lander—C. E.

Special thanks to the photographers and institutions that made *ZooBorns!* possible:

Anteater:
Jason Collier/Discovery Cove

Beco:
Grahm Jones
Columbus Zoo and Aquarium

Radar Ears:
Cherl Kim/Everland Zoo

Menari:
Audubon Nature Institute

Hoover:
Jason Collier/SeaWorld Orlando

Kai:
Dave Parsons/Denver Zoo

Amani: Mark M. Gaskill,
Phoenix Innovate,
taken at the Detroit Zoo

Miracle Kitten:
Shannon Calvert, taken at
Connecticut's Beardsley Zoo

Hasani:
George Nikitin,
taken at the San Francisco Zoo

Kali and Durga:
Robert La Follette,
taken at Tampa's Lowry Park Zoo

Rooby:
Darlene Stack/Assiniboine Park Zoo

Sasa:
Cheryl Piropato/
Fort Wayne Children's Zoo

Tahina:
Museum de Besançon

Monifa:
Lorinda Taylor/Taronga Zoo

Matari:
Lorinda Taylor/Taronga Zoo

Kalispell:
Dave Parsons/Denver Zoo

Bella:
Brenna Hernandez/Shedd Aquarium

BEACH LANE BOOKS * An imprint of Simon & Schuster Children's Publishing Division * 1230 Avenue of the Americas, New York, New York 10020 * Text and photograph compilation copyright © 2010 by Andrew Bleiman and Chris Eastland * All rights reserved, including the right of reproduction in whole or in part in any form. * BEACH LANE BOOKS is a trademark of Simon & Schuster, Inc. * For information about special discounts for bulk purchases, please contact Simon & Schuster Special Sales at 1-866-506-1949 or business@simonandschuster.com. * The Simon & Schuster Speakers Bureau can bring authors to your live event. For more information or to book an event, contact the Simon & Schuster Speakers Bureau at 1-866-248-3049 or visit our website at www.simonspeakers.com. * Also available in a Beach Lane Books hardcover edition * Book design by Lauren Rille * The text for this book is set in Century Schoolbook. * Manufactured in China * 0715 SCP * First Beach Lane Books paperback edition August 2015 * 10 9 8 7 6 5 4 3 2 * The Library of Congress has cataloged the hardcover edition as follows: Bleiman, Andrew. * ZooBorns! : zoo babies from around the world / Andrew Bleiman and Chris Eastland.—1st ed. * p. cm. * ISBN 978-1-4424-1272-9 (hardcover) * ISBN 978-1-4814-4702-7 (pbk) * ISBN 978-1-4424-3676-3 (ebook) * 1. Zoo animals—Infancy—Juvenile literature. I. Eastland, Chris. II. Title. * QL77.5.B54 2010 * 591.3'9073—dc22 * 2010009590

Do you like visiting baby animals

at zoos and aquariums? Then you'll love *ZooBorns!*

The newborn zoo critters in this book are cute and curious, and they enjoy exploring their world—just like you. But these babies are much more than sweet, furry faces. By allowing us to study them, zoo animals help us learn how to protect their wild cousins who live in jungles, deserts, mountains, and oceans around the world.

The more you know about animals, the more you too can help protect them. So turn the page and meet the ZooBorns. Then visit your local accredited zoo or aquarium to learn more!

Paul Boyle, Ph.D.

Senior Vice President for Conservation and Education
Association of Zoos and Aquariums

The Association of Zoos and Aquariums sets high standards to make sure all the animals at accredited zoos and aquariums get the very best care.

Hello there! I'm BECO, and I'm an
Asian elephant. When I grow up,
I'll be one of the largest animals
in all the land. But these days I'm happiest
rolling around with my big blue ball!

They call me **RADAR EARS**, and I'm a fennec fox. My big ears help me hear yummy insects crawling across the sand. Listen! Did you hear that?

My name is MENARI,

and I'm a Sumatran orangutan.

Check out my bright orange mop top.

There's no such thing as a bad hair day for me!

Hello, I'm **HOOVER**,

and I'm a tawny frogmouth.

They call me a frogmouth because of my beak.

I can open it *really* wide.

Calling all bugs . . . it's dinnertime!

I'm **KAI**, and I'm a spotted hyena.

Don't be fooled by my puppy-dog good looks—

we hyenas are more related to cats than to dogs.

Mom says I'm *purrrrrrr*fect.

My name is AMANI, and I'm an aardvark.

One day I'll grow into all this extra skin.

But for now, I think wrinkles rule!

Don't you?

I'm **MIRACLE KITTEN,**

and I'm an ocelot.

My teeth are starting to come in.

Want to see? *Ahhhhhhhhhhhhhhhh!*

Hi! I'm HASANI. I'm a gorilla,

and my name means "handsome" in Swahili.

The zookeepers say my name suits me well.

I think so too!

KALI and **DURGA** here!

We're Bengal tiger twins.

We look so much alike,

sometimes people can't tell us apart.

But we bet *you* can!

They call me **ROOBY**, and I'm a kangaroo.

What's a gal to do when her fur hasn't grown in yet?

Snuggle into this warm and fuzzy blankie—

that's what!

My name is **SASA**,

and I'm a banded mongoose.

The zookeepers say I'm a real rascal.

Do I look like trouble to you?

I'm **TAHINA**, and I'm a crowned sifaka.

When I was born, my mom couldn't take care

of me. So for now the zookeepers do.

They gave me this big teddy bear.

SO cuddly.

My name is MONIFA, and I'm a pygmy hippo.

We pygmies are the smallest hippos around.

But even though I'll always be little, I still have to

eat these leafy greens so I'll grow up strong.

Mmmmm.

G'day! I'm MATARI, a wombat.

I come from Australia,

where I love to dig in the dirt.

Check out the built-in shovels on my paws!

What do you get when you add a zebra's legs

to a giraffe's body—and then

throw in a long blue tongue?

Me! My name is **KALISPELL**,

and I'm an okapi.

Hello there. I'm an anteater,

otherwise known as a tamandua.

I was just born, and my mama hasn't named me yet.

Got any ideas for her?

And I'm **BELLA**, a beluga whale.

As I get older, I'll turn all white,

like my mom and dad.

But you know what will never change?

My smile!

Get to know the ZooBorns!

Name: BECO
Species: Asian Elephant
Home: Columbus Zoo and Aquarium, Ohio
Conservation Status: Endangered
Beco is the Columbus Zoo's second baby elephant. He loves to explore, splash in his pool, and play with his big blue ball. The largest land animal in Asia, these elephants are endangered due to habitat destruction.

Name: RADAR EARS
Species: Fennec Fox
Home: Everland Zoo, South Korea
Conservation Status: Least Concern
What's cuter than a fennec fox? Nothing! With impossibly oversized ears and a tiny body weighing only about 3 pounds (1.4 kilograms), even adult fennec foxes look like young pups. Their huge ears allow them to hear delicious insects scurrying around in the dark, while the thick tufts of fur on the bottoms of their paws protect them from the hot desert sand.

Name: MENARI
Species: Sumatran Orangutan
Home: Audubon Zoo, Louisiana
Conservation Status: Critically Endangered
The name Menari means "dance" in Indonesian—a fitting name for a great ape that swings gracefully from branch to branch among the treetops. Known for their intelligence, orangutans use tools to catch tasty termites and scrape stinging spines off their favorite fruits. There are only a few thousand Sumatran orangutans left in the wild.

Name: HOOVER
Species: Tawny Frogmouth
Home: SeaWorld Orlando, Florida
Conservation Status: Least Concern
While tawny frogmouths might look goofy, their fluffy feathers and spots help them stay amazingly well camouflaged. When roosting on branches, they look just like part of the tree! Tawny frogmouths are often confused with owls, but they are a different species. Like owls, they are night hunters. But unlike owls, they use their beaks rather than their talons to scoop up prey.

Name: KAI
Species: Spotted Hyena
Home: Denver Zoo, Colorado
Conservation Status: Least Concern
Spotted hyenas are among the most intelligent animals in the world, and current research compares them to great apes. Denver Zoo staff report that little Kai is particularly curious, smart, and adventurous. To avoid being picked up by his mother, he dives under logs and peeks out from below. He also enjoys exploring the smallest and most inaccessible areas in his habitat, jumping into the tall grass with his tail held high.

Name: AMANI
Species: Aardvark
Home: Detroit Zoo, Michigan
Conservation Status: Least Concern
Aardvarks might look silly, but their bodies are specially designed for seeking and snacking on their favorite food: termites! Oversized ears help aardvarks detect these insects, and their strong limbs and big claws help them dig up termites hiding deep underground. They use their twelve-inch-long extra-sticky tongue to slurp up the bugs—as many as 50,000 per night!

Name: MIRACLE KITTEN
Species: Ocelot
Home: Connecticut's Beardsley Zoo, Connecticut
Conservation Status: Least Concern
Fiercely territorial, ocelots like to be alone most of the time, but they occasionally rest in pairs on tree branches during the day. At night they head out to hunt, and their graceful, silent movement allows them to sneak up on small prey. The white circles around ocelots' eyes reflect light, enabling them to see exceptionally well in the dark.

Name: HASANI
Species: Western Lowland Gorilla
Home: San Francisco Zoo, California
Conservation Status: Critically Endangered
Hasani was his mother's first baby. She didn't immediately know how to care for him properly, so the zoo staff stepped in to raise the baby gorilla by hand. Shortly thereafter, they matched Hasani with another gorilla mother who loved him like one of her own.

Name: KALI and DURGA
Species: Bengal Tiger
Home: Tampa's Lowry Park Zoo, Florida
Conservation Status: Endangered
Contrary to popular belief, white tigers are not a separate species or albinos, but are typically Bengal tigers that carry an unusual gene that results in white coloring. Wild white tigers are very rare because their coats don't camouflage them in the forest, making it easy for their prey to see them.

Name: ROOBY
Species: Red Kangaroo
Home: Assiniboine Park Zoo, Canada
Conservation Status: Least Concern
After falling from her mother's pouch, little Rooby was lucky enough to be quickly rescued by zookeepers. The keepers were unable to determine which female had lost her joey, so they fashioned a fleece pouch for Rooby and successfully nursed her with a bottle. The largest of all kangaroos, red kangaroos can be found in nearly all parts of Australia.

Name: SASA
Species: Banded Mongoose
Home: Fort Wayne Children's Zoo, Indiana
Conservation Status: Least Concern
Sasa has four brothers, named Shangaza, Shitua, Sitini, and Shukuru, and one sister, named Sena. Banded mongooses have sharp little teeth, which they use for munching on the insects, lizards, and small rodents they dig up with their paws. Social critters, mongooses live in groups of up to 40, and they often sleep together in furry piles.

Name: TAHINA
Species: Crowned Sifaka
Home: Museum de Besançon, France
Conservation Status: Endangered
Crowned sifakas are a type of lemur. Like all lemurs, wild crowned sifakas exist only in Madagascar, which is an island off the southeast coast of Africa. Sifakas are most comfortable in the trees, but when they occasionally travel on the ground, they move in an amazing sideways hop. Threatened by deforestation, only about 1,000 sifakas are left in the wild.

Name: MONIFA
Species: Pygmy Hippo
Home: Taronga Zoo, Australia
Conservation Status: Endangered
While its larger cousin, the common hippopotamus, likes to lounge in the river and eat during the day, the shy little pygmy hippo doesn't mind being on dry land and only ventures out at night. For protection, some pygmy hippos even live in burrows along riverbanks like otters or muskrats! While living in a hole would be tough for their larger cousins, who can grow to 17 feet long (5.2 meters), pygmy hippos are only about 6 feet in length (1.8 meters).

Name: MATARI
Species: Common Wombat
Home: Taronga Zoo, Australia
Conservation Status: Least Concern
Matari means "little man" in Aboriginal. Like all wombats, Matari is mainly nocturnal, and he spent his first few nights playing in his pen until the wee hours, keeping his surrogate zookeeper mother wide awake. Since wombats are marsupials, Matari likes to spend some of his time in a pillowcase, which reminds him of his mother's pouch.

Name: KALISPELL
Species: Okapi
Home: Denver Zoo, Colorado
Conservation Status: Near Threatened
Little is known about the shy, mysterious okapi, which lives only in the dense Ituri Forest in central Africa. While the okapi's stripes make it look a bit like a zebra, this creature is actually most closely related to the giraffe. In addition to their dramatic markings, okapis have 14-inch-long blue tongues that enable them to grab tasty leaves that otherwise would be just out of reach.

Name: *Coming soon!*
Check ZooBorns.com to find out.
Species: Anteater (Northern Tamandua)
Home: Discovery Cove, Florida
Conservation Status: Least Concern
Anteaters *love* eating ants. In fact, they love eating ants so much, they can devour as many as 9,000 in a single day! For the first part of their lives, baby anteaters hitch rides on their moms' backs, going wherever Mom goes. When the babies are old enough to walk, they'll climb down to the ground and begin looking for ants on their own.

Name: BELLA
Species: Beluga Whale
Home: Shedd Aquarium, Illinois
Conservation Status: Near Threatened
Often called "canaries of the sea," beluga whales squeal, chirp, cluck, and whistle to one another as they swim. Shedd Aquarium's whales even mimic the sounds of the scuba divers who clean their habitat! Two layers of blubber keep wild belugas warm in the frigid Arctic waters where they live. Belugas can eat up to 80 pounds (36 kilograms) of seafood a day.